✝ CHRISTIAN PROGRAM

 Banyan   (954) 533-7705

950 N Federal Hwy Pompano Beach 33062

"Chaplain Anthony had a huge part in my recovery. . . . These devotionals have inspired so many 'God incidents' and shown so many people signs that helped with their recovery. As for me, it has taken away all questions and added to my faith in a way that will never be forgotten. A friend recently told me I'm a walking miracle because of the devotionals that inspired me to connect with God again and boosted my faith immeasurably."

—MATT PRINCE

"I knew the first day Anthony joined Banyan Treatment Center he would be a blessing! As our Program Director and Chaplain, he not only brought leadership skills to the program, but he has also provided us with great guidance and direction we need to make the program a success. He is truly a Man of God and his Daily Devotionals are truly impactful. The clients and I love them, and we look forward to starting our daily group sessions with them. The devotionals provide the clients with great comfort and hope that sobriety is attainable, especially knowing they have an all-knowing, all-powerful God, who promised He 'will never leave them or forsake them' (Deuteronomy 31:6)."

—JOAN BOWLA, MSW
Clinical Coordinator and Primary Therapist,
Banyan Treatment Center—IOP Christian Program

Impact Devotional Series

Impact Devotional Series

Adding Fuel to Your Faith

Anthony P. Acampora

RESOURCE *Publications* · Eugene, Oregon

IMPACT DEVOTIONAL SERIES
Adding Fuel to Your Faith

Resource Publications
An Imprint of Wipf and Stock Publishers
199 W. 8th Ave., Suite 3
Eugene, OR 97401

www.wipfandstock.com

PAPERBACK ISBN: 978-1-4982-8358-8
HARDCOVER ISBN: 978-1-4982-8360-1

Manufactured in the U.S.A.   2/22/2016

I dedicate this book to my sisters, Lisa Turcotte and Bonnie Acampora. During an extremely difficult period in my life they were the ones who were always there for me. They demonstrated amazing, unconditional love, compassion, and strength. They did not give up on me, and I know their many prayers were answered. There is no way to ever repay them for all they did for me, but hopefully, this dedication will be a small token of my appreciation.

"Tell me who your friends are and I will tell you who you are."

—PETER L. ACAMPORA

This was something my Father said to me many times while I was growing up in Connecticut. He was a devout Christian, amazing Father and friend who I truly miss. I also dedicate this book to my Dad - Peter L. Acampora. RIP Leeboy.

Love,
Tony

Contents

Acknowledgements

I want to thank the following people for all of their help and encouragement over the years:

First and foremost I want to thank my Lord and Savior, Jesus Christ. He is where my peace, strength, forgiveness, and destiny come from.

Rob Kauffman, who has been a great best friend and encourager to me since junior high school.

Jordan Berk, who I worked with for many years in New York City and California. He was my roommate in Bayside, Queens, New York, and has been one of my closest friends the past eighteen years. He is one of very few people I have ever met who shares my sense of humor.

Tali Waxman, who has been a great friend the past ten years. She has such a huge heart.

Lynn Dadio, who has been such an incredible source of inspiration to me.

Pastor Rick Reichadt, who encouraged me countless times over the past ten years. He has taught me so much on so many levels, in particular regarding spiritual warfare. He has been and continues to be a tremendous spiritual support in my life.

My nephew, Peter Daigle, who is wise beyond his years and has a heart of gold.

My brother-in-law, Mario Turcotte, who has helped me in many ways throughout the years. He is a truly generous and compassionate person.

International Evangelist John Ramirez and Champions Ministries Pastor Sandra Sarraga, who encouraged me to have the devotionals published.

Adriana Aycart-Ospina, who helped so much with the initial devotional edits. She has been a great friend and source of much encouragement.

Thanks to my editor, Clem Boyd, a real great guy, and probably the best editor since the guy who edited Hemingway. May God bless all of the above mentioned people, and I truly say thank you.

Introduction

I want to thank everyone who took the time to read these devotionals. It was truly a pleasure writing them. This series began as a result of a client's request while I worked as a chaplain in a treatment center. "I like the Bible verses that you talk about," she told me one day, "but I don't really know where to find them, or sometimes I do not fully understand them. Why don't you write something to explain the verses?"

And so *The Impact Devotional Series* was born! The devotions initially went to clients, then many mental health and recovery clinic staff members, police officers, firefighters, students, friends, hospital employees, and now, to you. It is so rewarding to hear that these writings have made an "impact" in the lives of readers, and, most importantly, that God allowed me to play a part in bringing others closer to Him.

I am very thankful for the incredible people at Wipf & Stock Publishers for publishing this book. If you would like to share how the devotionals affected you or someone you know, please visit the Facebook page *Impact Devotional Series*, or email me at aacampora3@gmail.com.

Until the next series, thank you, and God bless you and your family.

Anthony Acampora

Preparing to Use Your Impact Devotional

L ord God, I invite the Holy Spirit to speak to me though these devotionals. Please direct me to exactly what I need to read. Lead me now to the devotional that You have for me, which is in Your perfect will.

I now put my complete trust in You, Lord. Please have me open to the exact devotional that will reveal Your will for me on this day.

In Jesus' name I pray, Amen.

Following Instructions from Above

I will instruct you and teach you in the way you should go; I will counsel you with my loving eye on you.

—PSALM 32:8, NIV

Thought of the Day: Am I waiting on God's instruction?

Today's Devotional

Throughout God's word, we see He is a loving Father who wants to instruct, teach, and bless us. If we are going to be a recipient of these things, we must first seek Him. All of the benefits of the Father are there for us when we establish, or re-establish, our relationship with Him.

Heavenly Father, I give You thanks for the many blessings You have poured over me. Please continue to reveal Your perfect will.

In Jesus' name I pray, Amen.

Where Are The Other Nine?

As Jesus entered a village there, ten lepers stood at a distance, crying out, "Jesus, Master, have mercy on us!" He looked at them and said, "Go show yourselves to the priests." And as they went, they were cleansed of their leprosy. One of them, when he saw that he was healed, came back to Jesus, shouting, "Praise God!" He fell to the ground at Jesus' feet, thanking him for what he had done. This man was a Samaritan. Jesus asked, "Didn't I heal ten men? Where are the other nine? Has no one returned to give glory to God except this foreigner?" And Jesus said to the man, "Stand up and go. Your faith has healed you."

—LUKE 17:12-19, NLT

Thought of the Day: What am I grateful for?

Today's Devotional

Many times we blame God for what is wrong in our lives but never give Him thanks or show gratitude for what He has done for us. Maybe we take Him for granted because of the countless answered prayers and blessings. We learn from Luke 17 that God does, in fact, notice those who are ungrateful for the blessings He gives us. When we direct our focus on what we have, rather than on what we do not have, we will quickly realize we have much for which to thank Him.

Heavenly Father, I thank You for all of the amazing blessings that You have given me.

In Jesus' name I pray, Amen.

Anger: The Potentially Destructive Emotion

"Then the Lord said to Cain, 'Why are you angry? Why is your face downcast? If you do what is right, will you not be accepted? But if you do not do what is right, sin is crouching at your door; it desires to have you, but you must rule over it.'" Now Cain said to his brother Abel, "Let's go out to the field." While they were in the field, Cain attacked his brother Abel and killed him."

—GENESIS 4:6–8, NIV

Thought of the Day: Am I controlling my anger
or is it controlling me?

Today's Devotional

The first murder ever recorded—Cain and Abel. Many of us are familiar with this story. Cain kills his younger brother Abel. Why? Because he did the wrong thing with the offering, became angry and jealous of his own brother, and disregarded what God told him he must do. God told him. "Sin is crouching at your door." He warned Cain, but Cain did not listen, and the result was a tragic one. We can save ourselves much pain and suffering when we follow God's lead. Follow the peace and allow Him to direct your path.

Heavenly Father, I welcome Your instruction, guidance, and will for my life.

In Jesus' name I pray, Amen.

Come As You Are

Come to me, all you who are weary and burdened, and I will give you rest.

—MATTHEW 11:28, NIV

Thought of the Day: What is keeping me from trusting Him?

Today's Devotional

When we are covered in guilt and shame, it may be difficult to believe that Jesus would want anything to do with us, let alone give us rest. But that is exactly what He wants to do! 2,000 years ago, Jesus surrounded Himself with the worst people of the time. When questioned as to why, He replied, "It is not the healthy who need a doctor but the sick" (Matthew 9:12, NIV). What Jesus was saying is this: Come exactly how you are. He will transform your heart and mind and give you rest. He will give you the peace which surpasses all understanding.

Heavenly Father, Thank you for accepting me as I am and for replacing fear with peace.

In Jesus' name I pray, Amen.

The More I Trust God,
the Less I Fear My Situation

God has said, "Never will I leave you; never will I forsake you." So we say with confidence, "The Lord is my helper; I will not be afraid. What can mere mortals do to me?"

—HEBREWS 13:5-6, NIV

Thought of the Day: I have faith, so why am I afraid?

Today's Devotional

When we truly believe in our heart that God is with us, it really does not matter who or what is against us (Romans 8:31b). This requires us to step out in faith. As our faith increases, and we witness God's power, wisdom, and mercy, it becomes increasingly apparent that He is true to His word, and He has never left us, nor will He leave us.

Heavenly Father, I thank you for always being with me no matter what my situation. I trust in You above all. Please continue to protect me in all that I do.

In Jesus' name I pray, Amen.

Faith in The Midst of the Fire

These trials will show that your faith is genuine. It is being tested as fire tests and purifies gold—though your faith is far more precious than mere gold. So when your faith remains strong through many trials, it will bring you much praise and glory and honor on the day when Jesus Christ is revealed to the whole world.

—1 PETER 1:7, NLT

Thought of the Day: How can I grow through this trial?

Today's Devotional

Throughout our lives, we may have experienced tremendous adversity. Only after having victory over adversity are we then empowered, strengthened, and wiser from the experience. Although we may not like going through difficult situations, we must always remember that God will work all things together for our greater good, and He will turn our tests into our testimony.

Father, I thank You for the many times You have carried me through the storms. I ask for continued strength, direction, and wisdom.

In Jesus' name I pray, Amen.

Complete Trust in Him

Faith is the confidence that what we hope for will actually happen; it gives us assurance about things we cannot see.

—HEBREWS 11:1, NLT

Thought of the Day: How much do I truly trust God?

Today's Devotional

Faith is defined as complete trust or confidence in someone or something. Paul writes in 1 Corinthians 13:12, "All that I know now is partial and incomplete, but then I will know everything completely, just as God now knows me completely" (NLT). If we had full knowledge of God, there would be no need for faith. When we move from *some* trust in God to *complete* trust in God, we will be amazed how much closer to Him we are.

Father, I ask for an increase of faith and trust in You and in Your will for my life.

In Jesus' name I pray, Amen.

Where Do I Find Hope, Peace, and Joy?

May the God of hope fill you with all joy and peace as you trust in Him, so that you may overflow with hope by the power of the Holy Spirit.

—*ROMANS 15:13, NIV*

Thought of the Day: Am I trusting God with all my heart?

Today's Devotional

Jesus said in John 14:27, "Peace I leave with you; My peace I give to you" (NIV). He made it very clear that His peace is different from the peace offered by the world. Sometimes even knowing this, we still search for peace elsewhere, only to be continuously let down by people and circumstances we hoped would bring us peace. Put complete trust in Him and allow His hope, peace, and joy to overflow in your life.

Father, I ask for an increase of Your presence in my life.

In Jesus' name I pray, Amen.

Faith Throughout the Storm

But when you ask Him, be sure that your faith is in God alone. Do not waver, for a person with divided loyalty is as unsettled as a wave of the sea that is blown and tossed by the wind.

—JAMES 1:6, NLT

Thought of the Day: Am I really trusting Him?

Today's Devotional

We know from God's word that He releases His power and goodness in our lives as we live out our faith in Him. Hebrews 11:6 tells us that without faith it is impossible to please Him. This is particularly key in our prayer life. We may ask God for direction and to open doors to find a job, but then say something on Facebook or Twitter that shows we don't really believe God's going to respond i.e. "I'm never going to find work." Like fuel for a car, faith is the power that energizes our prayers.

Father, I thank You for all the times You have brought me through the storms in life. Please increase my faith and allow Your will to be done, not my will.

In Jesus' name I pray, Amen.

Tell Me Who Your Friends Are
and I Will Tell You Who You Are

Do not be misled: Bad company corrupts good character.

— *1 CORINTHIANS 15:33, NIV*

Thought of the Day: Who am I surrounding myself with?

Today's Devotional

We may have experienced peer pressure at some point, or we may be experiencing it now. We may have every intention of doing the right thing, but if we are continuously influenced to do the wrong thing by our inner circle, the outcome is usually not a good one. Surround yourself with those who speak life into you, offering encouragement and correction based on God's truth, and watch how things begin to change for the better.

Father, I ask for the right people to come into my life, people who are uplifting and encouraging. I ask for Your help and the strength to move away from those who are discouraging and destructive to my life.

In Jesus' name I pray, Amen.

His Will, Not My Will

The Lord says, "I will guide you along the best pathway for your life. I will advise you and watch over you."

—PSALM 32:8, NLT

Thought of the Day: Am I really trusting in God? Am I really seeking Him?

Today's Devotional

Through the prophet Jeremiah, in chapter 29, verse 11, the Lord says He has a plan for us, a plan to give us hope and a future. If we truly believe this, there is really no need to worry or fear during times of uncertainty or change. The more we draw close to God, the more we will realize this is true and He does have a plan for our lives. Allow Him to take the lead.

Father, I thank You for guiding and directing my paths. You are an anchor for my soul during difficult times. I ask for an overflow of Your presence.

In Jesus' name I pray, Amen.

Carried Through The Storms

The righteous cry out, and the Lord hears them; He delivers them from all their troubles. The Lord is close to the broken-hearted and saves those who are crushed in spirit.

—PSALM 34:17–18, NIV

Thought of the Day: "Where would I be without you?"

Today's Devotional

When we are going through the difficult and painful times in life, it is sometimes hard to comprehend that during such times God is closest to us. Only after we have gone through the hard times can we appreciate that God brought us through it. We may then have a better understanding of the last line in the *Footprints in the Sand* poem: "When you saw only one set of footprints, it was then I carried you."

Father, I thank You for all the times You have carried me through the storms in life.

In Jesus' name I pray, Amen.

Trust in God

The Lord hears his people when they call to him for help.
He rescues them from all their troubles.
The Lord is close to the brokenhearted;
he rescues those whose spirits are crushed.

—*PSALM 34:17-18, NIV*

Thought of the Day: Am I calling to Him for help?

Today's Devotional

Last night, I was looking through my journals from the past four and a half years. It was really amazing and very clear just how many times this Scripture actually happened. I confess, before I scanned my journal, I hadn't really noticed God rescuing me and helping me in my troubles. We sometimes remember what we perceive as unanswered prayers, or God not hearing us, yet fail to remember and appreciate all the times He has been there for us.

Father, I thank you for Your presence and for Your love, mercy, and grace. Thank you for never leaving me.

In Jesus' name I pray, Amen.

Seek Him First

Obviously, I'm not trying to win the approval of people, but of God. If pleasing people were my goal, I would not be Christ's servant.

—GALATIANS 1:10, NLT

Thought of the Day: Am I people pleasing or God pleasing?

Today's Devotional

Many times we are faced with doing something contrary to God's will in order to please people or to advance someone's agenda. God wants to fulfill the pure desires of our hearts because He is the one who gave us those desires. When we seek Him first, we allow ourselves to be blessed in ways that only He can bless us.

Father, I give you thanks for Your direction and the opportunity to learn more about You and Your ways. Please provide me with the strength to seek You with all my heart.

In Jesus' name I pray, Amen.

Choose to Trust Him

And we know that in all things God works for the good of those who love Him, who have been called according to his purpose.

—ROMANS 8:28, NIV

Thought of the Day: If I truly believe that God will work all things together for good, there is no need to worry.

Today's Devotional

During the storms in life, it is difficult to see how anything good can come of our trials, but God sees the big picture and wants to turn our test into our testimony. He wants to use our experience to help others going through similar struggles. He comforts us, so we can comfort others (2 Corinthians 1:4). Allow Him to use your suffering and experiences to reach others.

Father, I thank you for the plan you have for my life; please use me to be a light in a dark world.

In Jesus' name I pray, Amen.

Unforgiveness—The Spiritual Poison

*Never pay back evil with more evil. Do things in such a way
that everyone can see you are honorable. Do all that you
can to live in peace with everyone. Dear friends, never take
revenge. Leave that to the righteous anger of God.*

—ROMANS 12:17-19, NLT

Thought of the Day: Who have I not forgiven?

Today's Devotional

The definition of forgiveness is "surrendering the right to get
even." The key words are "the right," which means we were
in fact wronged, or hurt, however, we are making the choice to
give up the right to resentment. If we compare our suffering to
what Christ endured, we realize there is no comparison. Consider
the first thing He said from the cross: "Father, forgive them; for
they know not what they do" (Luke 23:34, KJV). There is no better
example of forgiveness than that. Begin to follow His example and
you will begin to experience His peace.

Father, I ask for the strength to be able to forgive those who hurt
me.

In Jesus' name I pray, Amen.

Give God the Glory He Deserves

I love the Lord, for he heard my voice;
he heard my cry for mercy.
Because he turned his ear to me,
I will call on him as long as I live.

—*PSALM 116:1,2, NIV*

Thought of the Day: Do you thank God
more than you blame Him?

Today's Devotional

Sometimes we pray for something, God answers the prayer, and we never bother to thank Him. Yet, we are quick to shake our fist at Him when our situation does not change. When Jesus healed the ten with leprosy, only one came back to thank Him. If you think He does not notice these things, take a look at Jesus' response: "Where are the other nine? Has no one returned to give praise to God except this foreigner?" (Luke 17:17b-18, NIV). Yes, it was only the Samaritan who gave thanks. Keep this in mind the next time your prayers are answered and when they are not answered!

Father, I thank you for all of the blessings You have already given me, the ones that I know of and the ones I do not.

In Jesus' name I pray, Amen.

Eternity

And God will wipe away every tear from their eyes; there shall be no more death, nor sorrow, nor crying. There shall be no more pain, for the former things have passed away.

—REVELATION 21:4, NKJV

Thought of the Day: Am I truly trusting where I will spend eternity?

Today's Devotional

We may have grown in some areas in our relationship with God, but often times when it comes to where we spend eternity, we sometimes waver in our faith. If you have ever lost a loved one, you may have a better understanding of what I mean. As we continue to grow in our faith and trust in God, we can begin to rejoice in His amazing *grace*!

Father, I thank you for Your *amazing grace*.

In Jesus' name I pray, Amen.

God Has A Plan For Your Life!

"For I know the plans I have for you," declares the Lord, "plans to prosper you and not to harm you, plans to give you hope and a future. Then you will call on me and come and pray to me, and I will listen to you. You will seek me and find me when you seek me with all your heart."

— JEREMIAH 29:11-13, NIV

Thought of the Day: Have I been seeking God?

Today's Devotional

The Bible tells us 88 times to *seek* God! In Hebrews 11:6, we are told that He rewards those who diligently *seek* Him (NKJV). Start this day to *seek* God with all your heart, and watch Him begin to work in your life.

Father, I thank You for the plan that You have for my life. Please, continue to reveal Your plan for me in Your perfect timing, as I seek You with all of my heart.

In Jesus' name I pray, Amen.

Trust Through the Turmoil

We can rejoice, too, when we run into problems and trials, for we know that they help us develop endurance. And endurance develops strength of character, and character strengthens our confident hope of salvation. And this hope will not lead to disappointment. For we know how dearly God loves us, because he has given us the Holy Spirit to fill our hearts with his love.

—ROMANS 5:3-5, NLT

Thought of the Day: How can I grow from every negative situation?

Today's Devotional

When we participate in exercise (weight training, running, swimming), we quickly realize that the more resistance we face, the more positive effect it has on our physical body. If we relate this to our daily life, the more we face resistance and trials, the stronger we become. Keep this in mind during the next difficult situation, and allow God to build your character and confidence.

Father, I put my trust in You alone during every situation, and I trust that You will work it together for good.

In Jesus' name I pray, Amen.

Prayer vs. Worry

Don't worry about anything; instead, pray about everything. Tell God what you need, and thank him for all He has done. Then you will experience God's peace, which exceeds anything we can understand. His peace will guard your hearts and minds as you live in Christ Jesus.

—PHILIPPIANS 4: 6-7, NLT

Thought of the Day: Prayer is something to be done *instead* of worry, not something done with worry.

Today's Devotional

When we pray about something and still continue to worry about it, we are demonstrating a lack of faith that God hears our prayer or that He will do anything about the situation we are praying about. By worrying, we are meditating on what is contrary to God's word. As we begin to worry less and trust in Him more, we will begin to experience His peace.

Father, I thank You for all of the blessings You have already given me. I trust in You and Your will.

In Jesus' name I pray, Amen.

Gratitude

I know what it is to be in need, and I know what it is to have plenty. I have learned the secret of being content in any and every situation, whether well fed or hungry, whether living in plenty or in want. I can do all this through Him who gives me strength.

— PHILIPPIANS 4:12–13, NIV

Thought of the Day: Where is your strength coming from?

Today's Devotional

For those of us who have dealt with tremendous loss in life, Paul's writings in Phil: 4:12–13 may provide a reminder of just how fortunate we are to have made it through various situations and trials. Often times, we realize much later that we were able to make it through, not by our strength, but His.

Father, I ask for an increase in gratitude and appreciation for all that You have brought me through. You are my strength.

In Jesus' name I pray, Amen.

Peace Instead of Fear

Peace I leave with you; my peace I give to you; not as the world gives do I give to you. Let not your heart be troubled, neither let it be afraid.

—JOHN: 14:27, NIV

Thought of the Day: Where are you trying to find peace?

Today's Devotional

In John 14:27, Jesus made it very clear that we will not find true peace in the things of the world (houses, people, cars, position, money). We try to fill a God-shaped hole with these temporary things, only to remain empty. In the second half of the verse, He says not to be troubled or afraid. Stand on this verse and replace fear with peace!

Father, I ask for the strength to stand in faith on John 14:27 through any future trials in my life.

In Jesus' name I pray, Amen.

Controlling My Thought Life

*Don't copy the behavior and customs of this world, but let
God transform you into a new person by changing the way
you think. Then you will learn to know God's will for you,
which is good and pleasing and perfect.*

—ROMANS 12:2, NLT

Thought of the Day: I will allow God to renew me on a daily basis.

Today's Devotional

Our thoughts play an enormous role in our lives. "As [a man] thinketh in his heart, so is he" (Proverbs 23:7, KJV). Interrupt the pattern of negative thinking and allow God to reveal His will for your life.

Father, I give You thanks for Your word and the opportunity to learn more about You and Your ways. Please provide me with the strength to practice what I have just learned.

In Jesus' name I pray, Amen.

Why Trust?

Trust in the Lord with all your heart,
And lean not on your own understanding;
In all your ways acknowledge Him,
And He shall direct your paths.

—PROVERBS 3:5-6, NKJV

***Thought of the Day**: Who am I putting my trust in?*

Today's Devotional

The Bible tells us to *trust* in God with all our heart. This does not mean "to a certain point." We are also told not to lean on our own understanding. The prophet Isaiah tells us in Isaiah 55:9 that God's ways are higher than our ways and His thoughts are higher than our thoughts. If we begin to truly trust in *the Lord*, He will direct our paths.

Father, I thank You for Your word. I humbly ask for an increase in my capacity to trust.

In Jesus' name I pray, Amen.

Seek God With All Your Heart

"For I know the plans I have for you," declares the Lord,
"plans to prosper you and not to harm you, plans to give you
hope and a future. Then you will call on me and come and
pray to me, and I will listen to you. You will seek me and find
me when you seek me with all your heart."

—*JEREMIAH 29:11–13, NIV*

Thought of the Day: Are we spending more time
with our problems or with God?

Today's Devotional

If we truly seek God with all of our heart, we will find Him. Hebrews 11:6 tells us that He rewards those who diligently *seek* Him. Start today, and seek God with all your heart.

Father, I give you thanks for the opportunity to draw closer to You.

In Jesus' name I pray, Amen.

Walking in the Spirit

But the Holy Spirit produces this kind of fruit in our lives: love, joy, peace, patience, kindness, goodness, faithfulness, gentleness, and self-control. There is no law against these things.

—*GALATIANS 5:22–23, NLT*

Thought of the Day: Is my response pleasing to God?

Today's Devotional

We will face the option of responding to a situation or person in a negative way. We can choose to walk in the Spirit by responding with "self-control" and "patience." This does not mean we allow ourselves to be taken advantage of, but we respond in a calmer and more controlled state of mind. Our point of view will be expressed more clearly and hopefully will be better received. By taking time to respond, we can reflect on the situation and then determine our role in it. When we realize that we played a part in the dispute, it will be much easier to understand the other person's point of view.

Father God, allow me to be more understanding and to respond to any situation in a manner that is pleasing to You.

In Jesus' name I pray, Amen.

Random Acts of Kindness

*For I was hungry, and you fed me. I was thirsty, and you gave
me a drink. I was a stranger, and you invited me into your
home. I was naked, and you gave me clothing. I was sick, and
you cared for me. I was in prison, and you visited me. Then
these righteous ones will reply, "Lord, when did we ever see
you hungry and feed you? Or thirsty and give you something
to drink? Or a stranger and show you hospitality? Or naked
and give you clothing? When did we ever see you sick or in
prison and visit you?"*

*And Jesus said, "I tell you the truth, when you did it to
one of the least of these my brothers and sisters, you were
doing it to me!"*

—MATTHEW 25:35–40, NLT

Thought of the Day: See people through the eyes of God.

Today's Devotional

Lately, when I encounter people who serve the underprivileged,
homeless, etc., Psalm 139:14 comes to mind: "I am fearfully and
wonderfully made" (NIV). I have been guilty of not being as kind as
I should be, but when I reflect on how precious we all are in God's
eyes, it really inspires me to make the effort to help those in need.

Father, I ask You to fill me with kindness, generosity, and love, so I
can pour it out on those in need of comfort.

In Jesus' name I pray, Amen.

Did God Really Say . . . ?

*Now the serpent was more crafty than any of the wild
animals the Lord God had made. He said to the woman,
"Did God really say, 'You must not eat from any tree in the
garden?'"*

—*GENESIS 3:1, NIV*

Thought of the Day: Who am I listening to?

Today's Devotional

From the beginning, the devil has been trying to deceive man-
kind; he is the master of deception. When we take our focus off
God and His direction, we can open the door to the enemy and his
evil ways. Keep your eyes on God, and let Him direct your path.

Father, I give You thanks for Your protection from the evil one.
I ask that You continue to guide and direct my path. I put all my
trust in You.

In Jesus' name I pray, Amen.

*This is the last devotional in this series. This is the only one in the series that I started from the devotional; all the others began with the quoted scripture. This happened without realizing it would be the last one. This is also probably the most personal devotional because it comes from a situation that just occurred the day before writing it.

Blessings to all,
Anthony

Avoiding The Trap

Do not be overcome by evil, but overcome evil with good.

—ROMANS 12:21, NIV

Thought of the Day: Am I responding
through God's will or my will?

Today's Devotional

It's so easy to fall into the enemy's trap, especially when responding to what we perceive as criticism. It just took me about 24 hours to see something for what it really was and not hold a grudge, yet address my role in the situation. When we truly see things through the eyes of others, and put ourselves in their shoes, it is much easier to forgive rather than harbor resentments.

Heavenly Father, thank You for Your direction through Your word and Spirit. Please allow me to always seek You before responding to any situation.

In Jesus' name I pray, Amen.